# Pay to Let US Go:
## Afrodescendants' Benefits and Costs to America

### Brooks B. Robinson

©Brooks B. Robinson
BlackEconomics.org
June 2012
Honolulu, Hawaii

Dedication

To the Most Honorable Elijah Muhammad who is the author of the most important literary work of the 20$^{th}$ century for Afrodescendants, *Message to the Black Man in America*.[1] In it he wrote:

- "We must stop relying upon the white man to care for us." (p. 170)
- "The day has arrived. He [the white man] has no more work for us to do. He is not willing to tell us that. The time has arrived when deep within his own heart he desires that you [Afrodescendants] go out and find a job for yourself. He will forever be burdened. The burden will get greater and greater as long as he tries to carry you and me." (p. 63)
- "So, therefore, we should look forward and try to get the government to agree to let us go somewhere by ourselves and build a nation of our own and on some of this land that we helped get." (p. 312)

Table of Contents

Preface ................................................................iv
Introduction .........................................................1
Section 1—Benefits ..............................................5
Section 2—Costs (Part I) ....................................15
Section 3—Costs (Part II) ...................................30
Section 4—Benefit-Cost Analysis .........................40
Conclusion ........................................................46
End Notes .........................................................48

**Preface**

As Maulana Ron Karenga once stated, "We don't live in the middle of the air. We live in a definite social and historical context." It is important to add that we live in an economic context; one in which costs and benefits are weighed and which informs our decisions and actions. This monograph seeks to provide an economic context for Afrodescendants' existence within the American context. It is just one of several works that we have put forward with the intent of helping Afrodescendants realize that we should strike out on our own and establish a new nation. For the first time, this work pulls back the curtain and shows US governments that the costs to maintaining Afrodescendants is high. It is a cost that may be too much to bear in the long run.

Our hope is that this work motivates Afrodescendants to recognize that we impose a high cost on American governments relative to the benefits that we provide. Those costs may be offset somewhat by other contributions that we make. Nevertheless, this work should enable us to realize that there is a way out.

Also, our hope is that the US Federal, State, and Local governments will use this work to see clearly the costs that Afrodescendants impose. In the long term, given the fiscal overhang that now prevails for all levels of US government, this cost picture may motivate these governments to look for a real and permanent solution. We conclude that that solution is separation and the founding of a new Afrodescendant nation.

In a world that is perceived to be increasingly resource constrained, warm and fuzzy notions about what we prefer must be juxtaposed against what is realistically feasible and against what is likely to work. It is difficult to imagine that the American society will continue to welcome an Afrodescendant group that sucks up an increasing volume of resources without contributing much to the pot. Therefore, it may be in everyone's best interest to simply *Pay to Let Us Go.*

**Introduction**

When the cost of maintaining an account exceeds the benefits derived from that account, it may be time to terminate the account. This is the proposition that confronts the US Federal, State, and Local governments. Afrodescendants function in the polity, earn income, and pay taxes. At the same time, like other groups in the polity, Afrodescendants cause these governments to incur costs. The unfortunate circumstances surrounding Afrodescendants' participation in the polity is that we generate a high level of costs relative to the benefits that we provide in the form of tax payments.

This monograph tackles this cost-benefit conundrum and presents analytical results that show the extent of the uneven burden that Afrodescendants place on US governments. Critics may argue that Afrodescendants provide the society much more than is accounted for by the taxes that we pay. We represent a core historical aspect of the American tradition and culture. We bring much enthusiasm and gusto when it comes to living the life that is America in the form of sports and entertainment. In fact, some Black critics may argue that Afrodescendant culture is the only uniquely American culture—in particular the culinary, musical, and literary contributions.

This may all be true. However, the accounts do not lie. Consequently, as US governments at all levels weigh the fiscal overhang that they confront now and in the future, they must decide how to begin to balance their books, or the entire house of cards will come tumbling down. When one has an unbalanced budget, there are clearly two sides of the ledger to consider. First, one can consider options to expand revenues. Given Afrodescendants' failings on the side of investment (mainly educational investment), and the correlation between that investment and the ability to produce income, it does not seem likely that Afrodescendants will raise proportionally our income and the related tax contributions. So then you turn to the other side of the ledger and look at expenses or, in this case, costs. The aforementioned Afrodescendant failings point to the likelihood that, in fact, Afrodescendants will engender increasingly higher costs to US government in the forms of high levels of unemployment, healthcare costs, and income security claims. What are these governments to do?

As budgets take center stage as we move through the 21$^{st}$ century, and governments fight to maintain their credit ratings by reducing imbalances, it is just a matter of time before politicians will begin to point to the role of Afrodescendants in exacerbating the imbalances. When this happens, other groups in the polity will begin to look unfavorably on Afrodescendants. But we are not in the 1940s where members of unwanted groups can be sent off to gas chambers. On the contrary, civil and human rights are uppermost in the hearts and minds of people all over the world. As a nation that wants to stand at the top of the world, the US will be hard-pressed to address this Afrodescendant benefit-cost problem effectively.

Hence, the efficacy of this monograph. The warning that it sounds awakens US governments to a future that can be avoided. We suggest that these governments curry an interest on the part of Afrodescendants to get off of the dime and decide once and for all the nature of our future. Will we all, to a citizen, agree that conformity is the order of the day. Or will we decide that there is good in the uniqueness of Afrodescendantness.

If the former, then we can expect to see Afrodescendants intermarrying with Whites, Asians, and Hispanics in an effort to join mainstream America with rising incomes, paying higher taxes, and creating fewer costs for the society. If the latter, then the best bet for US governments and Afrodescendants is a move toward separation.

In fact, there are strong arguments that individuals behave differently in new environments. In other words, it is possible that, if Afrodescendants were permitted to establish our own new nation, then we would behave differently. We might develop pride in the ability to control our own destiny, and adjust our thinking concerning what is important. We may find that it is possible to organize and operate an Afrodescendant nation successfully.

Where should such a nation be established and where are the resources that might be used to spark this new endeavor. Well, that is where US governments come into the picture. What we know from Biblical history is that the Israelites were given a grand send-off when they left Egypt. Therefore, it may be possible that the good people of the United States might see fit to permit their governments to create a good send-off for Afrodescendants as we undertake the formation of our own nation.

*Pay to Let Us Go* invites US citizens and governments to consider the future and to make a decision to assume the burden of what will be 60 million Afrodescendants or more by 2050, along with our limited tax contributions that are swamped by the very high costs that we will impose on the society. On the other hand, these citizens and governments can take action to shift that burden off the books and permit Afrodescendants to grow up as a people and as a nation.

Section 1 of this monograph begins by looking at the positive side of the ledger and assesses the benefits that Afrodescendants bring to the US. Section 2 begins a two-part presentation on costs. In Part 1, we discuss the theoretical and conceptual aspects of costs. In Section 3, Part 2 of costs, we dig into the numbers. First, we describe the methods that we will use to estimate those costs, and then we describe the estimation process and provide the results. In Section 4 we summarize by reviewing the benefit-cost analysis, highlight the imbalance in Afrodescendants' contributions to the US, and then forecast what the projected unfunded liability is likely to be over the next 25 to 50 years. Finally in the Conclusion, we provide final salient points on this very important topic.

**Section 1—Benefits**

Attempting to assess the total value or benefit of a group must be as difficult as trying to assess the value of a human life. The answers that are derived, in large measure, depend on those who are performing the assessment. Nevertheless, one can narrowly define one's purpose and make a determination based on that definition. If one remains true to that definition, then it becomes difficult to argue with the ultimate finding. In this case, we are seeking to identify the benefits that Afrodescendants bring to US governments in cash dollar terms. In other words, how many tax dollars do Afrodescendants place in government coffers? However, for sake of completeness of discussion, we analyze other areas where Afrodescendants provide benefits. For example, to what extent do Afrodescendants provide for the defense of the nation? What about the entertainment value of Afrodescendants who engage in athletics and other forms of entertainment. In an odd way, Afrodescendants provide benefits to the average non-Afrodescendant simply based on the fact that the latter's well-being may be enhanced by the realization that they are not, but Afrodescendants are, at the bottom of the socio-economic ladder in America. Of course, our entire purpose here is to lay out the benefits that Afrodescendants provide to US governments so that we can compare them with the related costs.

*Incomes earned*

It is important to begin this section with the realization that, for 2010, US gross domestic product (GDP) and the related income (gross domestic income (GDI)) were estimated by the US Department of Commerce's Bureau of Economic Analysis (BEA) at $14.5 trillion.[2] Unfortunately, this measure of output and income is not prepared on a "by race" basis. In fact it is very difficult to identify official comprehensive measures of Afrodescendant income. Consequently, we are faced with preparing estimates of the benefits that Afrodescendants provide to the wider nation based on a range of estimates that likely encompass the true value.

If we were to take a purely proportional approach to measuring Afrodescendants incomes, we would note that with a population of 42 million of "Black alone or in combination" citizens, Afrodescendants comprised 13.6% of the total 308.7 million US population in 2010.[3] Therefore, we could estimate that, at the outside, Afrodescendants might account for as much as 13.6% of the $14.5 trillion US GDI or $2 trillion. The reality is that we know that Afrodescendants' incomes are disproportionate with income of the broader American populace. On a household income basis, the Census Bureau's Current Population Survey reports that median household income for Blacks was $32.1 thousand compared with $49.4 thousand or about 65%.[4] In other words, based on disproportionality, we could conclude that US Afrodescendants may have earned about 65% of the $2.0 trillion or $1.3 trillion in income during 2010.

Notably, in 2011, we prepared a detailed analysis of US Afrodescendants' income for 2009. We concluded that US GDP would have been $1.2 trillion less had Afrodescendants not participated in the productive effort.[5] We determined that this level of income was not commensurate with the level of Afrodescendants' participation in the labor force. Nevertheless, it is a reading of how much income Afrodescendants earned, and it is a basis for determining how much taxes Afrodescendants paid. Of course, because we are performing our analysis for the year 2010, we must estimate similar values of

Afrodescendant income for that year. Given that the US economy grew substantially from 2009 to 2010, the expectation is that Afrodescendant income at market prices for 2010 should be above $1.2 trillion. Therefore, let us settle on the previously described estimate of $1.3 trillion as an upper-bound to Afrodescendants' income for 2010.

On the other hand, the Census's Bureau's Current Population Survey indicates that, in 2010, there were about 15.6 million "Black alone or in combination" households in the US, with a mean income of $45.2 thousand. That combination of statistics yields total income of $706.4 billion.[6] Similarly, the Bureau of Labor Statistics Consumer Expenditure Survey indicates that the 14.8 million consumer units in its sample had mean income of $45.7 thousand, for a total income for Afrodescendants in 2010 of $677.7 billion.[7] These are two key sources of statistics concerning Afrodescendants' income, yet they understate, for a variety of reasons, the value of income when computed using the methodology described in the two previous paragraphs.

Suffice it to say that US Afrodescendants' income for 2010 probably lies within the range of $675 billion to $1.3 trillion dollars. That is a wide interval, but we will use it for purposes of this analysis.

*Income for consumption*

Once one has generated income, there are mainly two options: Consume it or invest/save it for the future. In fact, Afrodescendants play a considerable role in bringing benefits to other US citizens by using our income for consumption and saving/investment purposes. This consumption spending creates jobs and incomes for other Americans, who can, in turn, use their consumption and saving/investment to create even more jobs and incomes. This "multiplier effect" of Afrodescendants' income produces benefits well beyond the income itself. Because it is not the focus of our analysis, we do not attempt to ascertain the magnitude of the multiplier effect here.

*A source of income*

Which sectors of the economy benefit most from Afrodescendants' presence in the US? This is an important question that warrants a study in and of itself. However, without being too precise, let's discuss a few areas where Afrodescendants appear to be disproportionately represented on the client side. Specifically, let us consider three areas of the economy that come to mind: Health; Public order and safety; and Income security.

On the one hand, experts argue that Afrodescendants receive poor quality healthcare in the US. Many of us cannot afford the healthcare that we need; others receive substandard healthcare. However, nearly 20% of US GDP is accounted for by healthcare, so Afrodescendants consumption of even a relatively small share of this sector of the economy accounts for a significant dollar value. On the other hand, it is also argued that, by waiting until a crisis unfolds before healthcare is sought, the cost of the healthcare received by Afrodescendants rises. Clearly, it is cheaper to stitch up a cut than it is to amputate a foot because the cut is not stitched up properly, becomes infected, and turns gangrenous. Therefore, from this perspective as well, Afrodescendants incur highly-valued healthcare services. As a result, we can surmise that Afrodescendants create the opportunity for a large volume of jobs and incomes in the healthcare services sector of the economy.

On June 30, 2009, According to the Bureau of Justice Statistics, 905,800 of the total 2,297,500 in custody in state or federal prison or in local jails were Black.[8] That is a 39.4% share; nearly three times the share (13.6%) of Afrodescendants in the US population  Each of these Blacks who were in custody required some form of legal representation, and many had their day(s) in court. Consequently we find that Afrodescendants contribute in a very large way to the "Public order and safety" sector of the US economy—creating numerous jobs and a high volume of incomes. Simply consider that legal counselors represent one of the highest paid professions in the US.

Finally on the Income security front, we are concerned with the role that Afrodescendants play in creating jobs and incomes for those who manage citizens who are on disability, who are retired, who receive welfare and social services, unemployment benefits, and other income transfers. As already intimated—and as will be highlighted in greater detail later in this monograph—Afrodescendants are disproportionately represented in certain Income security categories. Therefore, we play a major role in creating jobs and income opportunities for many non-Afrodescendant Americans.

*Taxes*

As in the case of income, there are no official comprehensive measures of the amount of taxes that US Afrodescendants pay. Therefore, we will use a few approaches to estimate the amount of taxes that are paid by Afrodescendants. Keep in mind that, from a US governments' perspective, taxes represent the benefits that they receive. As already mentioned, Afrodescendants may contribute to the society in other ways. However, for governments, the key benefit indicator is taxes paid.

Governments compare taxes paid with the costs incurred to assess balance, and then, ultimately, decide whether the benefits that they provide should be increased, held constant, or curtailed. We will address costs issues in Sections 2 and 3. For now, we focus on tax benefits.

An official measure of taxes paid by Afrodescendants, which is not comprehensive, is the value that comes out of the Bureau of Labor Statistics' Consumer Expenditure Survey (CES). The CES is related to personal household consumption, income, and taxes. The 2010 value from the previously cited Table 2100 may be derived from the fact that total estimated personal taxes were $214.3 billion and that Blacks or African-Americans accounted for 2.8% of those taxes, or about $6 billion. Clearly this number represents a huge understatement of Afrodescendant payment of taxes to Federal, state, and local governments.

Another approach is to consider national income and tax receipt aggregates, derive a ratio of total tax receipts to GDI, and then apply that ratio to the range of Afrodescendant income that we have estimated above. Consider Table 1 (next page). It shows that relevant US total tax receipts were $3.8 trillion in 2010, with GDI of $14.5 trillion, producing a tax-to-GDI ratio of 26.4%. We applied that ratio to the range of Afrodescendant income that we estimated above, to produce a range of tax payments of $178.2 billion to $343.2 billion. This comprises taxes for Federal, State, and Local governments. These are the estimates against which we will compare costs later in this monograph.

Table 1.—Derivation of Afrodescendant Tax Payments
(In $'s billions, except where noted)

| Tax Receipt and Income Categories | US Total | Afrodescendant High Estimates | Afrodescendant Low Estimates |
|---|---|---|---|
| **Total Tax Receipts*** | **3,834.5** | **343.2** | **178.2** |
| Current tax receipts | 2,648.7 | 237.0 | 123.1 |
| Contributions for social insurance | 991.7 | 88.8 | 46.1 |
| Current transfer receipts | 194.1 | 17.4 | 9.0 |
| **Total Income (GDI)**\*\* | **14,525.7** | **1,300.0** | **675.0** |
| **Estimated Ratio of Total Tax Receipts to GDI** | **26.40%** | **26.40%** | **26.40%** |

\*–From National Income and Product Account (NIPA) Table 3.1, BEA
\*\*–From NIPA Table 1.10, BEA
Shaded area represents author's estimates.

11

*Other important benefits*

Before concluding this section on benefits, it is important to highlight a few additional important benefits that Afrodescendants contribute to the American society. We are being very selective here; however, these are key areas that are often raised by Blacks and non-Blacks alike when seeking to assess Afrodescendants contributions. Specifically, we will discuss Afrodescendants' contributions in the form of: (1) Fighting in the defense of the nation; (2) Intellectual contributions or ideas; and (3) Entertainment contributions—athletically and in the performing, visual, and literary arts.

It may not be the case historically, but the US Department of Defense now reports near perfect proportional ethnic representation of its enrollment across the services: Army, Navy, Marines, Air Force, and Coast Guard. It may have been possible to contend in the past that Afrodescendants, because they comprised a disproportionate share of armed forces members of the lower ranks, died disproportionately for our nation. The reality is that today, ethnic groups generally serve and die in proportionate numbers across the board.[9] Importantly, while Afrodescendants cannot claim that we carry a disproportionate burden of the defense load, we can claim that we carry our equal weight.

Afrodescendants have always contributed to the formation of intellectual property in the US. Whether serving as assistants to primary developers of intellectual property, or being prolific contributors in our own right (e.g., Benjamin Banneker, Granville T. Woods, George Washington Carver, and Dr. Charles Drew), Afrodescendants have thought long and hard about how to make the nation function and produce more efficiently and effectively. In fact, the personal computer on which we are preparing this monograph, and the computers that now populate the global landscape are, in large measure, the result of inventions by an Afrodescendant—Dr. Mark Dean.[10] Too often, Afrodescendants who have developed intellectual property have been without the necessary financial capital to commercialize their inventions. Nevertheless, many of those inventions have been the source of millions of jobs and billions of dollars in income over the years. It is safe to say that the US would be much poorer than it is today had Afrodescendants not been a part of the nation's development. This is not to say that the inventions that are attributed to Afrodescendants would not have come along; just that they would have come along at a slower, more delayed pace. No question about it, Afrodescendants have benefited, and will continue to benefit, the US through intellectual property contributions.

Finally, consider Afrodescendants entertainment contributions through sports or the performing, visual, or literary arts. When we call the following selected names, great Afrodescendant entertainers/artists come immediately to mind: Jackie Robinson, Joe Lewis and Muhammad Ali, Nat King Cole, Wilt Chamberlain and Bill Russell, Jim Brown and Gayle Sayers, Arthur Ashe and Althea Gibson, Michael Jackson, Denzel Washington, Bill Cosby, Richard Wright, Maya Angelou, and Tony Morrison. Now consider how many additional great artists and authors that you know, and you come to realize that Afrodescendants have given so much to America. What you may also come to realize is that it was not just the special skill and grace that these entertainers brought to the fore that was so important, it was that by entertaining us with sport, singing, acting, or writing, they distracted our minds from the pain of living in America as part of an underclass. In many cases, these great entertainers assisted with the fight for "equality." However, their main objective, and the reason they were allowed to ply their trade, was that they transfixed us and took our minds off of the pain and anguish at hand. If they had not been so splendid with their crafts, maybe the US would not be standing as a nation today.

*Conclusion*

This section on the benefits that Afrodescendants bring to the US covers not only the important and calculatable incomes that Afrodescendants earn and the taxes that we pay to governments, but it also covers the very real benefits that Afrodescendants bring the nation in so many other ways. Afrodescendants are consumers and we represent disproportionate clientele to key professions that are able to create myriad jobs and vast incomes. Afrodescendants are willing defenders of the nation—although we no longer take up arms disproportionately. Very importantly, Afrodescendants assist the nation in remaining on the cutting edge of technological and human development by continuing to contribute to intellectual property formation and to entertaining the masses—in and outside of the nation.

These are all important benefits. However, the benefits that we are most concerned with here are those that reach governments. We will return to the estimates of taxes paid by Afrodescendants later in the monograph, after we have tackled cost issues.

## Section 2—Costs (Part I)

*Introduction*

If there is a defining theoretical economic concept that most non-economists know it is that "there is no such thing as free lunch." Interestingly, most non-economists also have internalized an appropriate and accurate interpretation of the concept; i.e., that there is a cost for everything. This section addresses the theoretical and conceptual costs that are associated with Afrodescendants' existence in the US. It is Part I on costs; Part II will delve into actual dollar estimates of the many costs that Afrodescendants impose upon the nation (see Section 3). In this part, we point out the fact that, theoretically and conceptually, it is often difficult to measure costs. We discuss the costs of existing in the US that are unique to Afrodescendants. We also identify costs that are imposed by Afrodescendants on the American society via the government. Finally, we turn our attention to a cost that is often ignored but always present—the cost of the potential threat.

*Difficult to measure costs*

It is important to realize that, from Afrodescendants' and Whites' perspectives, certain costs are difficult to measure. Certain costs that Whites impose upon Afrodescendants are difficult to measure, and certain costs that Afrodescendants impose upon Whites may be difficult to measure. We will consider one of the latter costs at the end of this section (the potential threat). Now, let us consider one of the former. Specifically, let us discuss "stress" as imposed upon Afrodescendants by Whites and the difficulty involved in measuring the impact of that stress.

When we say stress, what we really mean is fear. From the outset, because of the dastardly deeds that they planned to perpetrate on Afrodescendants, Whites knew that it was important to instill fear deep in the hearts and minds of Afrodescendants. They found innumerable ways to plant fear: Fear of death; fear of starvation; fear of rape; fear of all forms of physical torture and punishment; fear of an inability to obtain and receive love; and fear of having that love snatched away once it has been found. Today, many of these same fears are present in our world. The Trayvon Martin story is a case in point. The point being that these fears translate into low- and high-level stress depending on our life activities. This stress, in turn, causes physiological and biochemical changes in our bodies that are harmful to our existence.[11] When one combines the stress/fear from the past that was inbred in us through our mothers' wombs with the stress/fear that we experience today living in America, then one has a hellacious cocktail that raises our blood pressure, causes us to eat too much and brings on obesity, hypertension, insomnia, drug addiction, and so many other response behaviors that reduce our overall well-being.

When the doctor says high blood pressure (the silent killer), he looks for all types of causes. Is it your diet? Is it not enough exercise? Is it your relationships? He never asks, is it because you live in America as an Afrodescendant who is embroiled in a fearful and stressful environment that is imposed upon you by White America? You know that you are not trained to the going standard in substandard schools; therefore, you cannot perform to standard. You know that you cannot capture a well-paying job. You know that you do not have the expertise to start your own business. You know that unemployment benefits last only so long. You know that you cannot provide adequately for your family. You are in a Catch 22 and you do not know what to do. You are trapped. Most importantly, you know that you are consuming resources that White America would rather have for itself. All you know is that you are in the bowels of this nation with no way out. All the pressure is on you. All the stress and fear surrounds you and pervades your very being. You are a bomb ready to explode. But if you explode, you will be killed or certainly placed in prison. So you constrain yourself. You sit quietly and call for death. You only hope that life will be better for your children.

How do you measure the mental costs of the pain and the distraught nature of Afrodescendants who are caught in this situation? It boils down to the value of life, and it is difficult for anyone to place a value on a life. Who knows all of the potential that lies in a life? Maybe a great work of art is hidden there. Maybe inventions. On the other hand, it could simply be the importance of a spoken word to a child, who goes on to "save the world." It is difficult to measure.

Now let us consider a few direct costs that are obvious—not so difficult to measure.

*Costs unique to Afrodescendants*

There are certain measurable costs that Afrodescendants face during their sojourn in America. We do not attempt to measure them in dollars and cents, but by impact. They are unique to Afrodescendants and they are well known by us. We don't attempt to document these costs vigorously because they are so well known. They are mainly provided as a reminder to Afrodescendants of the unique burdens that we bear while living in America. They fall into "XXX while Black" categories.

**Studying while Black.**—Here we are having a phenomenon that arose following the desegregation of schools in the 1960s ad 1970s. The cost is imposed on at least two fronts. First, there is the distrust of teachers. When an Afrodescendant student produces an unexpectedly high-quality product in the classroom, there is the immediate disbelief that an Afrodescendant is capable of such high-quality work. Hence, the teacher instills within Afrodescendants a lack of self confidence. The teacher asks: "Did you do this?" "Who helped you?" "Where did you get this idea?"

Second, the slightest disruption in class turns into a suspension. Given sufficient suspensions, students then face expulsion. The National Association for the Advancement of Colored People (NAACP) has documented the problem of suspensions and expulsion of Afrodescendants students from schools in America. According to a 2009 report from the NAACP's Legal Defense Fund, 37.4% of all suspensions and 37.9% of all expulsions in the US during 2006 were accounted for by Afrodescendants, while Afrodescendants only comprised 17.1% of the elementary and secondary schools' population.[12] Do we have a problem or not?

Suspensions and expulsion lead to poor academic performance; to shame because students who are brought back into classrooms after suspensions are behind their peers; to frustrations; to fears/stress that they will be "left behind"; and ultimately to higher school dropout rates. Here we have a problem with a high cost.

**Driving while Black.**—While many scholars have written on the topic, Prof. Patrick Mason of Florida State University has written probably the most well-reasoned study on "Driving while Black." He concludes that there is clear evidence that police officers stop and engage in racially biased searches of Afrodescendant relative to their White counterparts on the roadway.[13] During the 1970s, 1980s, and 1990s, with a fastly accelerating drug culture in America, police justified their "vigilance" by arguing that Afrodescendants were disproportionately involved in the drug trade—which warranted a higher level of stops and searches. Of course, this was not true. Interestingly, stopping Afrodescendant along the roadway by security officials is a long-standing technique for Whites to keep track of Afrodescendant activities. Where are you going? What will you be doing in this area? Where are you from?

Imagine how many automobile accidents have been committed by Afrodescendants in their laudable efforts to get quickly to the roadside when a police vehicle pulls up behind or along side of them?

**Dying while Black.**—We need look no further than Prof. Vernellia Randall's 2006 book by the same title, *Dying While Black*, to uncover the many reasons why Black Americans die younger and at a disproportionate rate in the US healthcare system.[14] Suffice it to say that, as a result of Afrodescendants' living conditions in America we have a life deficit expectation. According to Dr. Randall, in 2002, life expectancy at birth for Afrodescendant males was 68.8 years, while it was 75.1 years for White males. For Black females, life expectancy at birth was 75.6 years, while it was 80.3 years for White females. (See Tables 02-04 and 02-05 in Dr. Randall's book; pp. 49-50.)

After living in America for over 400 years, and enjoying the many benefits that this great nation has to offer, why should there be a difference in life expectancy for Afrodescendants and Whites? Of course we know why. The point being that, while it may not be possible to place a value or cost on the years of life lost to Afrodescendants just for being who they are, we know that the years of life lost has an impact on the contributions that Afrodescendants could make to their community and to their family—with the latter contribution being the most important.

**Working while Black.**—If we were to delay the writing of this monograph a few years, it might turn out that this "XXX while Black" category might flip on its head. The sad fact is that in 2010, the Afrodescendant Unemployment rate was 16.0%.[15] The sadder fact is that there continues to be a precipitous decline in the Afrodescendant labor force participation rate. By April of 2012, while the Afrodescendant unemployment rate had fallen to 13%, it had only done so, in large measure, due to the fall in the Afrodescendant labor force participation rate, which had declined from 62.2% to 61.3%. At this rate, it is not difficult to imagine a point in the not too distant future where the labor force participation rate falls to below 50%. At that point, it will be easy to say that Afrodescendants are "hardly working."

When you combine the low labor force participation and high unemployment rates, you arrive at a situation where Afrodescendants are experiencing a tremendous amount of lost productive capacity. Think about how much better off our communities would be if more Afrodescendants were working and generating income. Consider how much more beautiful our homes, schools, and neighborhoods would be. For those Afrodescendants who are working, we have the everyday stress of having to perform at a higher level than our counterparts just to retain our jobs. On top of that, we have to be concerned with shielding ourselves from any wrong doing or innuendo: Theft, slothfulness, and sexual harassment. For some, everyday is a struggle with pressure/stress/fear. We leave home in the morning going to a job, not knowing whether we will return in the afternoon with our job still in hand.

A final point about Afrodescendants and our work is that we have clumped ourselves into a few industries, many of which have no long-term future. In 2007, we found that nearly 60% of Afrodescendants were in the following eight industries: (1) Retail trade (10.7%); (2) Educational services (8.6%); (3) Healthcare services, except hospitals (8.6%); (4) Transportation and warehousing (7.5%); (5) Public administration (6.7%); (6) Hospitals (5.9%); (7) Food service and drinking places (5.4%); and (8) Administration and support services (5.3%).[16] Most of these industries are of a variety that is declining in importance, and/or they are subject to being reorganized using high technology principles and practices. Now think about working a job with limited skills knowing that you are sitting on a ticking time bomb—it is just a matter of time before you are told that your services are no longer required because a computer or robot can do the work.

**Borrowing while Black**.—In the aftermath of the 2008-2009 global financial and economic crisis, we received the most recent round of criticism concerning Afrodescendant borrowing. The crisis provided grist for numerous studies showing how Afrodescendants were targeted by mortgage companies and were extended poor-quality loans; i.e., loans at higher interest rates than for which Afrodescendants qualified. While we do not cite these studies, we do cite a more general source from Ross and Yinger that highlights the cost imposed by Whites on Afrodescendants when it comes to borrowing.[17]

Whether it is mortgage loans, car loans, or student loans, it appears that Afrodescendants pay a higher cost to use other people's money. Obviously, it begs the question of why Afrodescendants do not organize ourselves and build our own banks from which we can borrow. However, that is a story worthy of a book by itself. What we know is that by paying more for loans, Afrodescendants ultimately have less resources to use to build our own lives, that of our children, and that of our communities. In the case of "Borrowing while Black," the cost is measurable, and the cost is high.

**Buying while Black**.—There are two important points to make with respect to this "XXX while Black" category. First, why should you accept an insult to spend your own money? In other words, Afrodescendants are often insulted just for browsing in a commercial establishment. Security personnel argue that they are concerned about theft. However, "guilt by color" is not the law of the land. Nevertheless, Afrodescendants endure these insults one day, and the next day find ourselves right back in the same store willing to endure the same insults again, just to give away our money for products that we could or should produce for ourselves. If Mahatma Gandhi could convince Indians to weave their own cloth and stop purchasing cloth from the British, why should not some Afrodescendant convince us to, at least as a starting point, buy the cloth and make our own clothes. All we need is a sewing machine. One day, maybe we can get around to weaving our own cloth. Ultimately, we might get around to growing our own cotton. You know, many years ago, we were pretty good at growing and picking cotton. Unfortunately, we do not seem to want to do that anymore. Of course, the key ingredient is that Afrodescendants must be certain to patronize our own businesses once we strike out on our own and begin to produce and sell our own products.

Second, even when Afrodescendants make an effort to avoid high markups on products and go to shopping malls and outlets, we still pay higher prices than Whites. Why? Because we usually reside further away from the malls and outlets than do Whites. Consequently, when transportation costs are factored in, we pay more for goods at the store than do Whites.

Therefore, whether it be paying the cost of insults or a higher prices, Afrodescendants accept the cost of "Buying while Black." It robs us of our dignity and of our cash; two things that we cannot afford to be without. Yet we struggle on here in America bearing the burden, and doing it gladly, instead of doing for self.

**Living while Black.**—There is only one key issue here, and that is the schizophrenia that results for Afrodescendants living in America. Afrodescendants have dual personalities: One for interaction with Whites and one for interaction with ourselves. God forbid that we forget which personality to use. It is not healthy. It is sick. Must we talk "proper" when we are with Whites? Must we wear clothes differently when we are with Whites? Must we eat differently when we are with Whites? We are stuck in an inverted conundrum trying to figure out which way is up. Should we act White or should we act Black? Be reminded that we cannot serve successfully two masters? We must love one and hate/despise the other. Do we know how to love ourselves? The cost imposed by this indeterminacy (Who do we love? Whites or ourselves) is the defining realization. When we are not accepted as we are—the product of those who made us who we are—then we must summon the courage to love ourselves despite ourselves, pick up ourselves, and move forward separately with ourselves to find a place of our own. The cost of failing to do this is the cost of failing to form a nation and be a

GREAT people. The cost of failing to do this is to be lost in history. The cost of failing to do this is the death of an entire nation of people.

We have captured and analyzed several of the "XXX while Black" cost categories. We do not reflect them all here. However, the costs that have been covered reflect the unique burdens that Afrodescendants now bear from living life day-to-day in America. The important questions to ask are, why should we continue paying these costs? How do we avoid paying these costs? How do we obtain reimbursement for the costs that we have paid? Responses to these questions are beyond the scope of this monograph. Nevertheless, we felt it import to remind Afrodescendants that there is a choice to maintaining the status quo. We leave it to readers to pursue answers to the question; i.e., to identify methods for upending the status quo.

*Costs imposed by Afrodescendants*

Now we consider, at least conceptually and theoretically, costs that Afrodescendants impose upon the larger, mainly White, society. We use as our framework of official categories established by the US Department of Commerce, BEA from two National Income and Product Account (NIPA) tables (3.16 and 3.17), which identify the key classes of expenditures made by Federal, State, and Local governments.[18] We consider each of the main categories that are presented in these tables, and discuss many of the subcategories. Here we discuss how and why Afrodescendants impose these costs. In Section 4, we will estimate the actual costs that Afrodescendants impose.

**General public service.**—Afrodescendants impose costs on the remainder of the society through all of the subcategories of spending: "Executive and legislative";

"Tax collection and financial management"; "Interest payments"; and "Other." Afrodescendants impose cost through the "Executive and legislative" subcategory because many sub-local governments are populated predominantly by Afrodescendants; therefore, a considerable volume of funds are utilized for the administration of these areas. Afrodescendants impose costs through the "Tax collection and financial management" subcategory because Afrodescendants are taxpayers and have our own proclivities to report and misreport; therefore, funds must be expended to bring Afrodescendants into compliance—just as other groups in the society must be. As for "Interest payments," Afrodescendants are assumed to contribute proportionally to the costs that warrant government borrowings and, therefore, are associated proportionately with the related interest payments. Finally, the "Other" category is comprised of miscellaneous spending for which Afrodescendants are assumed to be proportionally represented.

**National defense.**—We include this category here only to note that Afrodescendants do not impose a cost through "National defense." On the contrary, Afrodescendants contribute significantly to the defense of the nation. However, as a result of our participation in defending the nation, Afrodescendants become eligible to receive considerable amounts of social benefits that are made available through the Veterans Administration. Those costs are accounted for in several of the categories that are to be discussed below.

**Public order and safety.**—As discussed in Section 1 under the topic "A Source of income," Afrodescendants comprised a 39.4% share of persons in Federal, State, and Local prisons and jails in 2009. Consequently, it is no secret that Afrodescendants impose a high cost on the nation through all facets of the criminal justice system: Police and security officers, the courts, and the incarceration system. This is not to infer that all of these costs are justified, just that they are imposed. In addition, fire and rescue services are provided to Afrodescendant communities—probably on a proportional basis.

**Economic affairs.**—This category encompasses a variety of subcategories and mini-subcategories, which represent a variety of services that are provided by Federal, State, and Local governments. On the surface, certain subcategories, such as "Space," appear somewhat unrelated to costs that Afrodescendants impose on the society. However, in the final analysis, as members of the society Afrodescendants benefit from generally all of the "Economic affairs" functions and, therefore, impose our share of the costs through the production of the services.

**Housing and community services.**—The costs imposed by Afrodescendants through this category are transparent. Afrodescendants consume housing and community services; therefore, costs generated by the production of these services are attributable, in part, to us. Notably, the housing services that are provided to Afrodescendant Veterans are captured in this category.

**Health.**—As noted in Section 1, health comprises a large proportion of the total output of the US economy. Federal, State, and Local governments pay for a large proportion of total health expenditures, including those that are associated with health services being provided to Afrodescendants. Again, health services that are provided to Afrodescendant Veterans are reflected in this category.

**Recreation and culture.**—It goes without saying that Afrodescendants produce many of the services that are accounted for under this category. At the same time, Afrodescendants consume their share of these services and, thereby, impose costs for their production.

**Education.**—Logically, Afrodescendants consume educational services at the elementary, secondary, and higher education levels and impose costs accordingly. Veteran educational benefits that are consumed by Afrodescendants are accounted for in this category.

**Income security**—This category contains subcategories for those who are disabled, retired, or otherwise unable to care for themselves and require some form of income transfer. Many Afrodescendants fall into this category (e.g., those receiving welfare or social services and those who are unemployed), and impose the related costs on the broader society.

These eight categories (excluding "National defense") will be examined in greater detail in Section 3 (Part II of costs), when we dig into the numbers and actually estimate the costs that Afrodescendants impose.

*Cost of potential threat*

At the outset of this Section, we discussed costs that are difficult to measure. There we focused on a cost that is imposed by Whites on Afrodescendants that is difficult to measure—stress. Here we feature a cost that is imposed by Afrodescendants on Whites that is also difficult to measure. It is appropriate to discuss this cost by noting an important quote from Thomas Sowell in his voluminous work, *Intellectuals and Society.* Sowell quotes Ulrich Bonnell Phillips who, when it comes to racism in America, interprets the nation's condition aptly: "We do not live in the past, but the past in us."[19]

Many Afrodescendants do not know or have run away from our history (sometimes it is painful to know the entire truth), but Whites know what they have done to us. They have the records. They know the names—meaning they know the beatings, the rapes, and the tortures. They used religion to tame us and make us willing servants who love their masters. However, they also know that, just as it has happened in the past and will continue to happen in the future, there will be one who rises up and reminds the children of the crimes committed against them and calls them to seek justice. This threat always hangs over the head of White America. White America is always watching and listening and training spies to report those who might rise up to call for justice. That is why so many Afrodescendant males are in jail. That is why so many young Afrodescendant males and females are on psychotic medications. That is why so many Afrodescendants have been convinced that they are sissies—with no will to fight for justice and freedom. Whites live in the present, but the past haunts them. They make every effort to protect themselves from their past.

Afrodescendants have become a troublesome species of property: No longer needed for production, yet there is no quick method for dispensing with us. Importantly, every plan that has been tried to destroy us has failed. The final plot is to absorb us and make us nonexistent. That is a cost that is too high to pay for a people who survived the trek from Central Africa, the horrors of the middle passage, over 200 years of murderous chattel slavery, one hundred years of Jim Crow lynching slavery, and now nearly 70 years of an effort to absorb us into Whiteness outright. We have stood the test of time, we will continue to impose costs, and we will break the bank and the nation, or be set free—allowed to exit through a sea of red ink to the promised land. Afrodescendants have and will continue to play a role in bankrupting America, to the point where the nation will have no choice but to let us go.

While this plot is underway, Whites must continue to look over their shoulders every moment of the night and day. They must continue to check with their spies. However, despite their efforts, one will still rise to call Afrodescendants to seek freedom and justice. Will those that rise commit sabotage? Will they use their intellects in cyberspace to disrupt transportation and communication networks? Will they poison the water? Will they obtain a weapon of mass destruction? Will they submit to suicide bombs to snuff out the lives of business and political leaders who have stood in the way of our freedom and justice? What will we do? What cost will we impose? These are the questions that preoccupy the mind of White America. This preoccupation is the imposition of a cost that is difficult to measure. Only White America can tell us how much they expend in bearing this cost; how many sleepless nights; how many haunting moments. Their fear is that their past will be visited upon them.

## Section 3—Costs (Part II)

*Introduction*

What costs do Afrodescendants impose on the American society? What burden is imposed by Afrodescendants on Federal, State, and Local governments? This is the fundamental question that we are responding to in this monograph. In Part I of cost (Section 2), we contemplated costs in conceptual and theoretical terms. In this, Part II of cost, we crunch the numbers to arrive at a cost that we can juxtapose against taxes paid (see Section 4) to identify the net burden that Afrodescendants impose on US governments.

There are a few important points worth noting about this effort. First, we will employ an estimating process that is somewhat imprecise. Therefore, although there are separate estimates of total government spending by Federal and State and Local categories, we do not work at that level of detail. We operate at the macroeconomic (aggregate) level in our analysis as a sign of the imprecision involved.

Second, we take a conservative approach during the estimation process in an effort to not overstate the costs that Afrodescendants impose. Our hypothesis is that Afrodescendants impose a higher cost to governments than we pay in taxes. To avoid achieving self-fulfilling prophecy, we remain conservative in our approach. What this means is that we are likely to understate, at the margin, the total amount of costs imposed by Afrodescendants. In our estimation, it is better to arrive at such a conclusion than to over state the case.

Third, we make every effort to describe our estimation methodology so that others can replicate our approach should the inclination arise. We view this monograph as a document that can help initiate a conversation on Afrodescendants' costs to society with a set of facts in hand. Others may want to test our estimates and arrive at their own to extend the conversation. We provide estimation methodology details so that interested parties can do just that.

We begin this section with a general description of our methods, and then drill down and estimate Afrodescendants' costs on a spending category-by-category basis. We close this section with a conclusion, and then take up the benefit-cost analysis in Section 4.

*Methodology*

The basic methodology that we employ to estimate costs imposed by Afrodescendants on US governments is to identify total spending values from the US Department of Commerce Bureau of Economic Analysis (BEA) on a functional basis, and then to use statistics from other sources to develop what we determine are the shares that Afrodescendants account for of that spending.[20] The spending values are from National Income and Product Account (NIPA) Tables 3.16 (Current Expenditures by Function, lines 1-41) and 3.17 (Selected Government Current and Capital Expenditures by Function, the Gross Investment portion, lines 98-107).[21] In this way, we combine values from these two tables to identify total current spending for functions for 2010—current operational and programmatic and investment. We use a variety of sources and techniques in order to determine Afrodescendants' shares. We identify these sources and the techniques as we consider each function; i.e., category or subcategory of spending.

*Cost by Function*

We identified the eight functions (excluding "National defense") that we will assess here in Section 2. Readers are invited to return to that section in order to grasp the conceptual and theoretical reasons why we have concluded that Afrodescendants impose costs with respect to these functions or spending categories. Now we turn our attention to estimating actual costs by explaining our methods and deriving cost values.

**General public service**

Current expenditures on "General public service" in 2010 were valued at $680.7 billion, and Gross investment spending for the category was $36.3 billion. Current expenditures are allocated to the following subcategories: "Executive and legislative," "Tax collection and financial management," "Interest payments," and "Other." We distribute Gross investment spending according to the distribution of Current expenditures. For each subcategory, we assume that Afrodescendant spending is proportional to population. That is, we assume that spending for these subcategories that is associated with Afrodescendants is equivalent to Afrodescendants proportion in the US population.[22] We call this the "population share" method. Therefore, $93.5 billion of the total $717 billion expended on "General public services" is assigned to Afrodescendants; i.e., 13.045%.

**National defense**

We do not prepare estimates of the Afrodescendant share of "National defense spending" because, in fact, it is assumed that national defense would be provided for even in the absence of an Afrodescendant population in the US. As noted in Section 2, we concur that Afrodescendants help provide for the defense of the nation in a significant way. However, Afrodescendants do not impose a cost on the nation with respect to the provision of this function of government.

**Public order and safety**

Current expenditures for this function of government are presented in four subcategories: Police, Fire, Law courts, and Prisons. The value of Current expenditures for 2010 was $325.3 billion. Gross investment expenditures for this category was $19.2 billion. Gross investment spending was distributed to the four subcategories in accordance with their distribution of Current spending for the category. For the Police, Law courts, and Prisons subcategories, we assume that Afrodescendants accounted for a proportion equivalent to their representation in the Prison and Jail population.[23] For the Fire subcategory, we assume that Afrodescendants account for a proportion of that spending that is equivalent to our proportion of the US population. Therefore, of the $344.5 billion expended on "Public order and safety," we estimate that Afrodescendants account for $123.6 billion, or 35.874%.

**Economic affairs**

We estimate Afrodescendant costs for this function of government at a three broad subcategory level of detail: Transportation, Space, and Other economic affairs. In each case we assume that the best approach to estimating the cost that Afrodescendants impose is to adopt a proportional "population share" approach. Current expenditures for these three subcategories totaled $316.7 billion in 2010; Gross investment spending was $155 billion, which was distributed proportionally across the three Current expenditure subcategories. In other words, of the $471.7 billion expended on "Economic Affairs," we estimate that Afrodescendants impose 13.045% of the cost or $61.5 billion.

**Housing and community services**

This function/category of spending is presented in NIPA Tables 3.16 and 3.17 as one line item; $44.2 billion for Current expenditures and $53.8 billion for Gross investment. The category represents spending for housing development, community development, water supply, street lighting, etc. Consequently, we concluded that the "population share" approach was best suited for estimating costs imposed by Afrodescendants. That is, Afrodescendants imposed "Housing and community services" costs based on our proportion of the population. Therefore, Afrodescendants accounted for 13.045% of the total ($98 billion) cost imposed, or $12.8 billion.

**Health**

This function/category, too, was presented as one line item in the aforementioned NIPA Tables. However, we concluded that we should use two methods for estimating the health costs that Afrodescendants impose on the larger society. First, we decided to split the total cost of healthcare (Current expenditures of $1,091.7 billion and Gross investment of $23.7 billion for a total of $1,115.4 billion) into two components: Medicare and Medicaid.[24] The Medicare portion generally is associated with costs imposed by the aged in our society. The Medicaid portion generally is associated with costs imposed by the poor and indigent. Therefore, we distributed total health spending across Medicare and Medicaid subcategories using data for this spending from NIPA Table 3.12.—Government Social

Benefits (the Medicare expenditure estimate is on line 6, and Medicaid expenditure estimate is on line 33 of the table).

The second step is to identify the proportion of Medicare and Medicaid health expenditures to allocate to Afrodescendants. For Medicare, we obtained the proportion of aged US citizens that Afrodescendants represent. We determined this proportion by computing the share of Blacks who were 65 years of age or older (3,391 thousand) of the total population that was 65 years of age or older (39,571 thousand), or 8.569% (the "Aged share" method).[25] For Medicaid, we obtained the proportion of those in poverty in the US that are represented by Afrodescendants in 2010. We determined this proportion by computing the share of Blacks in poverty (10,675 thousand) of the total poverty population in the US (46,180 thousand), or 23.116% (the "Poverty share" method).[26]

Therefore, of the total Federal, State, and Local government spending on "Health," $166.8 billion is associated with costs imposed by Afrodescendant (14.953%).

**Recreation and culture**

Afrodescendants' imposition of "Recreation and culture" costs were estimated using the "population share" method. The category/function was presented as one line item in NIPA Tables 3.16 and 3.17. Current expenditures were $31.2 billion for 2010; Gross investment spending was $8.8 billion. We estimated Afrodescendants costs for this category at 13.045% of the total ($40 billion), or $5.2 billion.

**Education**

Current expenditures ($764.7 billion) for this function/category were presented in three subcategories: (1) Elementary and secondary; (2) Higher (Post secondary); and (3) Libraries and other. We allocated Gross investment spending ($87.5 billion) for this category across the three subcategories based on the Current expenditure distribution. We determined the Afrodescendant shares for these three subcategories in the following way:

- For Elementary and secondary, we identified the proportion of the total US Elementary and Secondary public school population that was accounted for by Blacks (16.8%).[27]
- For Higher (Post secondary), we identified the proportion of the total US Post Secondary population that was accounted for by Blacks (13.775%).[28]
- For Libraries and other, we used the "population share" percentage (13.045%).

Therefore, of the total Current expenditures and Gross investment for Education in 2010 (852.2 billion), 15.844% or $135.0 billion is estimated as the cost imposed by Afrodescendants.

**Income security**

NIPA Table 3.16 presents Current expenditures for the category/function ($1,305.3 billion) in five subcategories: (1) Disability; (2) Retirement; (3) Welfare and social services; (4) Unemployment; and (5) Other. We allocated Gross investment spending ($3.9 billion) across the five subcategories using the distribution that was reflected in the Current expenditures. We determined the costs imposed by

Afrodescendants for these five subcategories using the following methods:

- We used the "population share" method for Disability.
- We used the "Aged share" method for Retirement (see the Health category above).
- We used the "Poverty share" method for Welfare and social services (see the Health category above).
- For "Unemployment," we determined the proportion of Afrodescendants who were unemployed during 2010 as a share of the total Unemployed population in the US (15.642%).[29] However, because it is known that Afrodescendants generally earn less than others in the population, we factored down the Afrodescendant unemployment proportion using the ratio of Black median income to national median income (64.855%).[30]
- We used the "population share" method for "Other."

Therefore, of the $1.309.1 billion expended by Federal, State, and Local governments for 2010 for "Income Security," Afrodescendants are estimated to have imposed $170.3 billion of these costs or 13.011%.

*Conclusion*

This section, Part II of cost, provides an estimate of the portion of total Federal, State, and Local governments Current expenditures and Gross investment that is associated with costs imposed by Afrodescendants. Critics may argue that we have under- or over-estimated at the margin. However, we have attempted to use the most straight-forward approaches to parsing total expenditures into those that are accounted for by Afrodescendants and the proportion that is accounted for by the remainder of the US population. We have not employed any particularly clever approaches, but have resorted to tried and true methods for estimating shares. Because we have documented our work well, critics can take up the gauntlet and perform their own estimates and compare them with the ones that we have produced here.

Table 2 on the next page provides a summary of our findings. After excluding "National defense," we find that all levels of US government spent $4,947.9 billion on eight key functions of government. This spending represents spending for staff, operations, programs, new structures, equipment, etc. As the table shows, $768.8 billion of that spending is estimated to be associated with spending to meet Afrodescendants requirements. This represents 15.538% of total spending.

In Section 4, we will compare these estimated costs with the benefits that Afrodescendants provide the nation in the form of taxes paid. We will also show how the related cost-benefit deficit might evolve over the next 25-to-50 years. The question that we all should ask is, "Can the nation afford to continue to bear the burden that Afrodescendants impose?"

Table 2.—Current Expenditures and Gross Investment:
National Total and Afrodescendant Shares, 2010
($'s Billions)

|  | National Totals | Expenditures for Afrodescendants | Shares |
|---|---|---|---|
| **Total** | **4,947.9** | **768.8** | **15.538%** |
| General public services | 717.0 | 93.5 | 13.045% |
| Public order and safety | 344.5 | 123.6 | 35.874% |
| Economic Affairs | 471.7 | 61.5 | 13.045% |
| Housing and community services | 98.0 | 12.8 | 13.045% |
| Health | 1,115.4 | 166.8 | 14.953% |
| Recreation and culture | 40.0 | 5.2 | 13.045% |
| Education | 852.2 | 135.0 | 15.844% |
| Income security | 1,309.1 | 170.3 | 13.011% |

Source: National Totals are from BEAs; Expenditures for Afrodescendants are estimated by the author. The shaded area represents the author's estimates.

## Section 4—Benefit-Cost Analysis

*Introduction*

This monograph addresses three fundamental questions: (1) What are the benefits that Afrodescendants bring to the American society in the form of taxes paid? (2) What costs do Afrodescendants impose on the American society in the form of governments' expenditures? (3) Because the costs exceed the benefits by a sizeable margin, what should the nation do with respect to the large and increasing liability of retaining Afrodescendants in the nation?

This section reviews the benefits that were derived in Section 1 and the costs that were derived in Section 3. We compute the Afrodescendant burden as the difference between the two. Finally, we ask, "What should the nation do concerning this burden?" While we do not provide a detailed analysis of the options available to the nation to address the burden, we suggest one alternative that is worthy of consideration.

*Benefit*

In Section 1, we considered the conceptual and theoretical benefits that Afrodescendants bring to the nation—some easily measured, others not so easily measured. However, our main focus in the section was to estimate the incomes and taxes paid by Afrodescendants. When it was all said and done, we provided a range of incomes and taxes paid for consideration. According to our analysis, Afrodescendants earned in 2010 income in the range of $675 to $1,300 billion. Using the average effective tax rate for the nation, we estimated that Afrodescendants paid taxes in the range of $178.2 billion to $343.2 billion.

Of course, this is a very wide range of income and taxes paid. Going forward, we will use the top-end estimate for our analysis. In other words, we will assume that Afrodescendants paid at least $343.2 billion in taxes. This is the benefit that Afrodescendants brought to the table in the form of taxes paid to Federal, State, and Local governments. It is this figure that matters when policy makers are considering the benefits that a particular group provides. They juxtapose this benefit against the costs that the group imposes on the society.

*Cost*

In the previous Section 3, Part II of costs, we undertook a systematic effort to estimate the proportion of total government costs that are associated with meeting Afrodescendants' requirements. We concluded, as a point estimate, that of the total costs to Federal, State, and Local governments of $4,947.9 billion in spending, Afrodescendants imposed a cost of $768.8 billion. In other words, Afrodescendants accounted for 15.538% of the total costs (excluding "National defense"). This appears to be a reasonable estimate of costs because Afrodescendants ("Black alone") account for 13.045% of the US population, and it stands to reason that the nation would spend disproportionately to meet our needs given our history and our attendant problems that span a wide breadth of issues.

Nevertheless, it also stands to reason that the nation would, at some point, expect Afrodescendants to carry our own weight in the society. When will this become a reality for Afrodescendants? This is, in fact, the crux of the matter.

What are the prospects that Afrodescendants will overcome our hurdles and become equal participants in the society?

*Afrodescendant Burden*

This brings us to the point of identifying the fiscal overhang, as a burden. To the extent that Afrodescendants extract more in the form of costs than we contribute in the form of benefits (taxes paid), then the difference is a burden to society. If we perform the simple subtraction ($768.8 billion - $343.2 billion), we arrive at a burden for 2010 of $425.6 billion. In other words Afrodescendants costs represented 224% of the benefits that we provided in the form of taxes paid.

As noted above, this fiscal overhang may be acceptable for a period of time when a society has a significant surplus. However, in today's world of ballooning government deficits, it becomes increasingly problematic for society to support the burden of a group that perpetually extracts more in costs than it provides in benefits. Sooner or later, the society must address this structural imbalance. It must decide on how to manage such a large unfunded liability.

At least three questions are in order here: (1) Should the nation spend more to assist Afrodescendants in overcoming the conditions that prevent us from earning higher levels of income so that we can pay a higher level of taxes to offset our costs? (2) Should the nation find a way to cut costs so that the costs are more in line with the taxes that we pay? (Such cuts would have to be draconian in nature to create balance in the accounts.) (3) Should the nation seek to rid itself of the problem group altogether so that the fiscal overhand no longer exists?

*Growth of the Burden*

If the nation fails to address the issue immediately, then what is the likely outcome? Without a concerted effort to address the burden either from the benefit or cost side, the burden is likely to grow. We realize that the economy is becoming increasingly sophisticated and relies on cutting-edge technologies. How can Afrodescendants, who contribute and participate so sparingly in the fields of science and technology, grow our incomes and our taxes paid. On the other side of the ledger, how can Afrodescendants who are so mired in a Hip Hop culture of violence and sex, with minimal emphasis on high academic achievement, reduce our costs to the nation in the form of criminal justice, healthcare, and education? The most logical answer is that little progress will be made on either front. Consequently, the burden is likely to continue to grow. How rapidly? If we assume that growth of the Afrodescendant burden will keep pace with the Afrodescendant population growth rate, then we can compute how rapidly the burden will grow.

According to the 1910 to 2010 Decennial Censuses, the average growth rate of the Afrodescendant population has been 1.39% over the 100-year period.[31] If we begin in 2010 with a $425.6 billion Afrodescendant burden, and grow it 25 years at the 1.39% growth rate, we arrive in 2035 with an annual burden that is $601.0 billion. Cumulatively, the burden will have amounted to $13.2 trillion.

If we take a longer time horizon, using the same growth rate, and extrapolate the 2010 burden out 50 years, we arrive in 2060 at an annual burden that has reached $848.7 billion. Cumulatively, over the 50-year period, the burden would be valued at $31.3 trillion.

Figure 1 provides a graphical image of the estimated Afrodescendant burden to the American society over the next 50 years.

Figure 1.—Estimated Afrodescendant Burden, 2010-2060

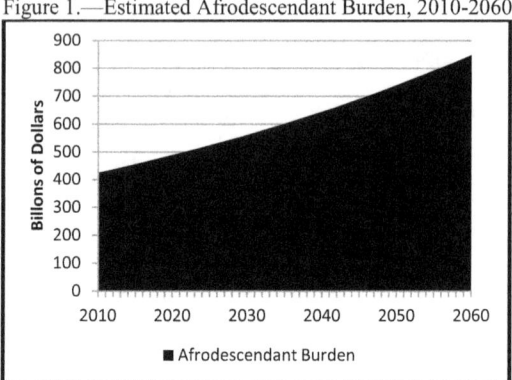

Source: Estimates from the author.

Clearly, this is an obvious burden that the nation needs to consider. It appears illogical to allow such a runaway burden to persist.

*What Should the Nation Do?*

Consistent with our historical efforts at BlackEconomics.org, we suggest that the US address the Afrodescendant burden by facilitating an exit of this troubled group. It is logical that Afrodescendants would grow up as a people and develop a sustainable nation on our own. It makes sense that a change of environment would produce a change in character, such that Afrodescendants would assume the duties and tasks of governance reliably. We would educate ourselves, create jobs for ourselves, and feed and protect ourselves. In this way, Afrodescendants would remove ourselves as a burden from US governments. However, the US would face the small matter of assisting Afrodescendants in identifying a land location for a new nation, and of providing a package of resources that would enable us to initiate our nation. Clearly, all of this does not come without a cost to the US, but the cost incurred for this option is likely to be considerably less than bearing the Afrodescendant burden over the next 50 years.

*Conclusion*

This section has brought together the estimated benefits and costs that Afrodescendants bring to the US in the form of taxes paid and costs imposed. The related burden is large—especially when considered over the next 50 years. However, the US has a reasonable option that removes the burden from its consideration, and it would help to give birth to a new nation—something that is very logical because the 40 plus million Afrodescendant population clearly constitutes a nation within a nation.

In the Conclusion, we recap this monograph by making a few remaining salient points about the Afrodescendant burden to US governments.

**Conclusion**

There is no free lunch! Afrodescendants and the rest of America must realize that we live in a resource-constrained world. Therefore, consumers are expected to compensate producers for the products that they consume. Producers must consider the price that they draw from the consumers of their products so that a profit is generated. At the same time, governments must consider the taxes paid (benefits) that they receive from groups within the society that impose costs (expenditures), so that fiscal balance or surplus can be achieved. No group can expect to consume/impose costs forever without, at some point, providing tax benefits that are at least equal to the cost imposed. Afrodescendants and US governments are in for a wake-up call because the Afrodescendant burden (costs less taxes paid) is too much to bear.

Policy makers may hide this conclusion fearing that it is not politically correct to speak out about it. However, rest assured that some interest group(s) in the American society will bring the issue to light. They will say flatly that Afrodescendants consume far more than they compensate: Government expenditures to meet Afrodescendants' requirements are far more than the taxes that Afrodescendants pay. The interest group(s) will do the math and conclude that this burden is too onerous to bear.

There is hope and there is a strategy. Afrodescendants can find a place where we are more productive and where we can pay our way. However, this place is likely to be outside of the American context. We have argued that "the past lives in us"; therefore, we need to identify a new environment, which can assist us in modifying our behavior. The establishment of an Afrodescendant nation could instill sufficient pride within us to study harder, get smarter, and work harder to build a stable society that does not result in deficits but in surpluses. However, we may require help in establishing this new national territory and in initiating production processes. There are numerous literary works that suggest how much the US should give to grant Afrodescendants a good sendoff and we recommend that they be consulted to resolve this issue.

In Section 4 we highlighted the estimated magnitude of the Afrodescendant cumulative burden over the next 50 years ($31.3 trillion). This burden is too large for the US to bear. Yet, given the status quo, it is unlikely that sufficient change will occur to reduce the cost of this burden if no action is taken to change the course of history. Knowledge of such a burden will cause interest groups in the society to find a way to dispense with the burden—some of which are not likely to be favorable. Therefore, Afrodescendants should take it upon ourselves to suggest real change now—nation formation—before the situation gets out of control.

At about the middle of the 19$^{th}$ century, President Abraham Lincoln and his cohorts had a similar idea. They formulated the Chiriquí Plan, but Afrodescendants rejected it. Now look at the outcome that rejection of that plan produced. What we know is that we cannot go on this way; therefore, we must resurrect something akin to the Chiriquí Plan and opt to move on in history to create new opportunities for Afrodescendants to show our inherent greatness.

In simplest terms, the US government and many of its citizens are likely to find that it is simply best to *Pay to Let Us Go*.

## End Notes

[1] Elijah Muhammad. *Message to the Blackman in America*. Secretarius MEMPS Ministries. Phoenix, Arizona. (1965)

[2] Bureau of Economic Analysis. "National Income and Product Account (NIPA) Table 1.1.5 (Gross Domestic Product) and 1.10 (Gross Domestic Income)." US Department of Commerce. Retrieved from the Internet on June 12, 2012; http://www.bea.gov.

[3] US Census Bureau. *The Black Population: 2010 (2010 Census Brief)*. US Department of Commerce. (September 2011). Retrieved from the Internet on June 12, 2012; http://www.census.gov/prod/cen2010/briefs/c2010br-06.pdf.

[4] Carmen DeNavas-Walt, Bernadette Proctor, and Jessica Smith. *Income, Poverty, and Health Insurance Coverage in the United States: 2010*. U.S. Census Bureau, Current Population Reports, P60-239. US Government Printing Office: Washington, DC; p. 6. (September 2011)

[5] Brooks Robinson. "Blacks' Role in the US Economy: 2008-9." BlackEconomics.org. (February 12, 2011). Retrieved from the Internet on June 12, 2012; http://www.blackeconomics.org/BE&Lit/BRITE.pdf

[4] Op. cit. (DeNavas-Walt, Proctor, and Smith). "Table A-2. Households by Total Money Income, Race, and Hispanic Origin of Householder: 1967-2010." (p. 36)

[7] US Bureau of Labor Statistics. *Consumer Expenditure Survey*. Table 2100.—Race of Reference Person. US. Department of Labor. (September 2011). Retrieved from the Internet on June 12, 2012; http://www.bls.gov/cex/2010/share/race.pdf.

[8] Heather West. *Prison Inmates at Midyear 2009—Statistical Tables*. Bureau of Justice Statistics. (June 2010). Retrieved from the Internet on June 12, 2012; http://www.bjs.gov/content/pub/pdf/pim09st.pdf.

[9] These conclusions are based on data that we received from the US Department of Defense, and which we would be happy to share with readers upon request.

[10] See "Dr. Mark Dean Computer Inventions" at the Internet Web site: *Famous Black Inventors*. Retrieved from the Internet on July 12, 2012; http://www.black-inventor.com/Dr-Mark-Dean.asp.

[11] Vickie Mays, Susan Cochran, and Namdi Barnes. (2007) "Race, Race-Based Discrimination, and Health Outcomes Among African Americans." *Annual Review of Psychology*: Vol. 58; pp. 201-225.

[12] NAACP Legal Defense & Education Fund, Inc. (2009) *Annual Report of the NAACP Legal Defense and Educational Fund, Inc. (2007-2009)*. p.43. Retrieved on June 12, 2012; http://naacpldf.org/files/publications/NAACPLDF_2007-2009_Annual_Report.pdf.

[13] Patrick Mason. (2007) "Driving While Black: Do Police Pass the Test?" *Swedish Economic Policy Review*: Vol. 14; pp. 79-113.
[14] Vernellia Randall. (2006) *Dying While Black*. Seven Principles Press, Inc. Dayton, OH.
[15] US Bureau of Labor Statistics. "Table A-2. Employment Status of the Civilian Population by Race, Sex, and Age." *Current Population Survey*. US Department of Labor. Retrieved on June 11, 2012; http://www.bls.gov/cps/cpsatabs.htm. .
[16] These statistics were obtained from the US Bureau of Labor Statistics. "Employed Persons by Race, Hispanic Origin, and Industry, 2007 Annual Averages." US Department of Labor.
[17] Stephen Ross and John Yinger. (2002) *The Color of Credit: Mortgage Discrimination, Research Methodology, and Fair-Lending Enforcement*. MIT Press: Boston.
[18] Bureau of Economic Analysis. NIPA Tables 3.16, "Government Current Expenditures by Function," and 3.17, "Selected Government Current and Capital Expenditures by Function." US Department of Commerce. Retrieved June 2, 2012;
http://www.bea.gov/iTable/index_nipa.cfm.
[19] Thomas Sowell. (2011) *Intellectual in Society*. Basic Books: New York. p. 122.
[20] Government spending by function is a concept that is promulgated by the International Monetary Fund (IMF). See the IMF's *Government Finance Statistics Manual 2001*, p. 76, Table 6.2: Classification of Expense by Function of Government. Retrieved from the Internet on June 16, 2012;
http://www.imf.org/external/pubs/ft/gfs/manual/pdf/all.pdf.
[21] Op. cit. (BEA, NIPA Tables).
[22] The population estimates are from the US Census Bureau and represent the population as of July 1, 2010. Total US population and "Black Alone" are available from the table "Annual Estimates of the Resident Population by Sex, Race, and Hispanic Origin for the United States: April 1, 2010 to July 1, 2011." Retrieved from the Internet on May 30, 2011;
http://www.census.gov/popest/data/national/asrh/2011/index.html .
Our use of the "Black alone" population category serves to keep our estimates conservative. A larger share would be derived if we used another Black related population category.
[23] Op. cit. (West). *Prison Inmates at Midyear 2009*. As noted in Section 1, of the 2,297,500 persons enrolled in Federal and State prisons and Local jails on June 30, 2009, Afrodescendants accounted for 905,800 or 39.425%.

[24] Our research of Center for Medicare and Medicaid Services (CMMS) did not reveal a share of Medicare enrollees who are Black for 2010. We identified a study of Medicaid enrollees for 2010 that covered 47 states. The share of Black enrollees produced by that study is not very different from the share estimate that we derive. Generally, the literature appears to reflect concern about the quality of CMMS data on the ethnicity of enrollees in both the Medicare and Medicaid programs.

[25] US Census Bureau. "Table 4, Annual Estimates of the Resident Population by Race, Hispanic Origin, Sex and Age for the United States, April 1, 2000 to July 1, 2009." US Department of Commerce. Retrieved from the Internet on June 16, 2012; http://www.census.gov/popest/data/historical/2000s/vintage_2009/index.html. At the time of this writing, data for 2010 were not available.

[26] Op. cit. (DeNavas-Walt, Proctor, and Smith). "Table 4. People and Families in Poverty by Selected Characteristics: 2009 and 2010." (p. 15).

[27] National Center for Education Statistics. "Public Elementary/Secondary School Universe Survey." US Department of Education. Retrieved from the Internet on June 16, 2012; http://nces.ed.gov/programs/digest/d11/tables/dt11_094.asp.

[28] National Center for Education Statistics. "Fall Enrollment Survey." US Department of Education. Retrieved from the Internet on June 16, 2012; http://nces.ed.gov/programs/coe/tables/table-gre-2.asp.

[29] US Bureau of Labor Statistics. "Table A-1. Employment Status of the Civilian Population by Sex and Age" and "Table A-2. Employment Status of the Civilian Population by Race, Sex, and Age." US Department of Labor. Retrieved from the Internet on June 11, 2012; http://www.bls.gov/webapps/legacy/cpsatab1.htm and http://www.bls.gov/cps/cpsatabs.htm.

[30] Op. cit. (DeNavas-Walt, Proctor, and Smith). "Table 1. Income and Earnings Summary Measures by Selected Characteristics: 2009 and 2010." (p. 6).

[31] US Census Bureau. "Decennial Censuses. US Department of Commerce. Retrieved on May 30, 2012; http://www.census.gov.

www.ingramcontent.com/pod-product-compliance
Lightning Source LLC
Chambersburg PA
CBHW061519180526
45171CB00001B/246